The BOYS' Book of Greatness

Book of Greatness

EVEN MORE WAYS TO BE THE
BEST AT EVERYTHING

Written by Martin Oliver
Illustrated by David Shephard
Edited by Hannah Cohen
Designed by Zoe Quayle

The BOYS' Book of Greatness

EVEN MORE WAYS TO BE THE
BEST AT EVERYTHING

SCHOLASTIC INC.

New York   Toronto   London   Auckland   Sydney
Mexico City   New Delhi   Hong Kong   Buenos Aires

No part of this publication may be reproduced, stored in a retrieval system, or transmitted in any form or by any means, electronic, mechanical, photocopying, recording, or otherwise, without written permission of the publisher. For information regarding permission, write to Michael O'Mara Books Limited, 9 Lion Yard, Tremadoc Road, London SW4 7NQ, United Kingdom.

Library of Congress Cataloging-in-Publication data available.

ISBN-13: 978-0-545-13408-8
ISBN-10: 0-545-13408-0

First published in Great Britain in 2008 by Buster Books, an imprint of Michael O'Mara Books Limited, 9 Lion Yard, Tremadoc Road, London SW4 7NQ, United Kingdom.
www.mombooks.com/busterbooks

Text and illustrations copyright © 2008 Buster Books

Cover design by Angie Allison (from an original design by www.blacksheep-uk.com)
Cover illustration by Paul Moran

12 11 10 9 8 7 6 5 4 3 2 1   9 10 11 12 13 14/0

Printed in the U.S.A.
First American edition, August 2009

NOTE TO READERS

CONTENTS

HOW TO PLAY AIR GUITAR

You've got the looks of a rock god
and you've got matching attitude to
boot. Unfortunately, you haven't
saved up enough for a real guitar
yet. Don't worry – air guitar
is the one instrument everyone can afford
and anyone
can play.
Here's how.

MASTERING THE
BASICS

1. Grab your air guitar.
Put the strap around
your neck and adjust so
it is at the right height
for you to play comfortably. Strike some poses in front of
a mirror to decide whether you want the guitar to sit high
up, level with your hips, or lower down, level with your
thighs.

2. Practice strumming. This is the key action for any air
guitarist. If you're right-handed, strumming is done by
moving your right hand up and down over the "strings,"
with your palm facing in toward your body. For a
variation, you can pretend that you're holding a pick,
which is a small triangle-shaped tool used for plucking the
strings individually or strumming.

3. Next practice your chord playing. Chord playing is when you play several notes at once. To do this, press down two or more fingers of your left hand firmly against the neck of your air guitar. Move your hand down the neck for high chords and up the neck for lower chords.

4. Select your music. Find a track with long guitar solos so you can really show off your skills. Listen to the track over and over again until you know it by heart. Practice strumming in time to the music, moving your hands up and down the neck to play the high and low parts of the track.

5. Start to move your whole body, including your head, legs, hips, and shoulders. Really get into it.

ADVANCED AIR GUITAR

As you get more confident, start adopting some more extreme poses. Don't be shy. Remember, the more energetic you are when playing, the better. Think about jumps, splits, and playing the guitar over your head or behind your back. You could even consider smashing the guitar at the end of your performance.

ROCK GOD

A costume will make your performance more authentic. Watch your rock heroes on TV or on the Web and copy what they're wearing. Add ripped jeans and a bandanna (simply tie a handkerchief around your forehead). Then pop on some shades and you'll be a true air-guitar rock legend.

HOW TO PITCH A TENT

Nothing beats the feeling of crawling out of the rain into your tent after a hard day of hiking in the great outdoors. Here are some tips to prepare you for pitching your tent like a pro.

THE PERFECT PLACE TO PITCH

• Look for a spot to put up your tent well before it gets dark. If you're not staying at an official campsite, ask permission before pitching your tent.

• Choose a site that is not in a valley or a ditch. If you choose either of those places and it rains, your tent could flood.

• Choose a spot that is sheltered from the wind. If you pitch your tent on an exposed area or on the top of a hill, you and your tent may risk being blown away!

• Choose somewhere as flat as possible. If there is a slight slope, it's best to make sure you sleep with your head higher than your feet.

• Check for any signs of animal tracks or insects. Camping on an ant nest could result in a serious case of "ants in your pants."

PITCHING THE TENT

Each tent is different — some tents will pop up by themselves, while some require poles and rain flies. Therefore, it is essential that you practice pitching your tent in a backyard or park before an overnight

expedition. Get familiar with how your tent works so you can put it up quickly when night is falling and time is short.

Never leave home without making sure all the pieces of your tent are in the bag and the instructions are packed.

When pegging out the ground sheet, make sure it is stretched out as flat as possible. Use a rubber mallet to hammer the metal pegs through the loops. If you have a separate ground sheet, always make sure that it is tucked up inside the tent to ensure that no water can get in.

When your tent is up, peg down the guy ropes so your tent is standing up without any creases. (Guy ropes are the ropes on the outside of the tent.) When you're putting the pegs into the ground, put them in at an angle of 45 degrees, leaning away from the tent. The ropes should pull on them at an angle of 90 degrees.

If it looks like rain, slacken the guy ropes slightly. This will reduce the chance of the pegs being dragged out of the ground or the tent material tearing in a heavy rain shower.

STRIKING YOUR TENT

When it's time to take your tent down (this is known as striking your tent), always pick up the ground sheet first. Turn it upside down to allow it to dry, and brush off any grass or dirt.

Pull the pegs out of the ground one by one. If you struggle to pull your tent pegs out, tap them back and forth with the rubber mallet to loosen them.

Try to dry your tent before packing it away. If you have to pack it up wet, dry it as soon as possible or it may get moldy.

Warning: Before you leave to go camping, make sure you tell an adult where you are going. Always carry a cell phone on an expedition so you can let an adult know where you are at all times, but realize that some campsites may not have cell-phone reception.

HOW TO MAKE A TANGRAM

Tangrams are a type of puzzle invented long ago in ancient China.

You will need to cut up a square of stiff cardboard into seven sections as shown here.

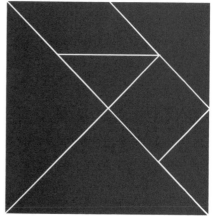

The object of a tangram puzzle is to rearrange the seven pieces of the square into different shapes to form a recognizable image. It is incredible how many shapes you can make using just the seven pieces of cardboard.

To start you off, here are some shapes that you can make by rearranging the pieces you have cut out. When you've done these, see how many more shapes you can make.

A rabbit sunbathing

A person cleaning a car

A person relaxing in the backyard

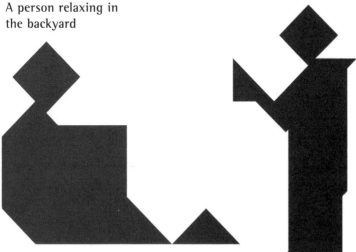

HOW TO BOIL AN EGG

If you want to be sure you never starve, learn how to cook a delicious soft-boiled egg. You could even impress your parents by making them a boiled egg with toast for breakfast in bed. Always remember to ask an adult before using the stove, and be careful around hot surfaces.

BE PREPARED

Take your eggs out of the fridge about twenty minutes before you boil them. If you take eggs straight from the fridge and put them into boiling water, they might crack.

If you forget to take your eggs out of the fridge in time and you are in a hurry, run them under warm water for a minute.

Don't choose really fresh eggs to boil, as you will find that their shells are hard to peel off once they are boiled. Instead choose eggs that are roughly five days old.

Find a saucepan just large enough for the eggs you want to boil. If you use a pan that is too large, your eggs may move around and crack against one another or on the side of the pan.

WHAT YOU DO

1. Pour some cold water into the saucepan. Bring the water to a boil.

2. Put a small pinprick in each of the eggs. This allows

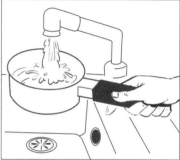

any steam to exit and will prevent cracking.

3. Place each egg on a spoon and gently lower it into the saucepan.

4. Reduce the heat so the water is no longer boiling but simmering (bubbling gently).

5. Set your timer. The length of time you cook the eggs depends on how you (or your parents) like them.

Timing: If you are using large- or medium-size eggs, cook your eggs for exactly three minutes. This will give you a perfectly cooked egg with a deliciously runny yolk. If you are boiling extra-large eggs, five minutes' cooking will leave the yolk runny. Seven minutes will mean the yolk will be slightly runny.

6. Once the cooking time is up, carefully pick up each egg with the spoon and place each one in an eggcup, with the rounder end of the egg at the bottom.

HOW TO SURVIVE AT SEA

Imagine you're on a leisurely sail, when suddenly your boat begins to sink. The gently lapping sea instantly becomes a treacherous ocean. In order to survive, you are going to need skill, endurance, luck, and the following tips.

STAY ONBOARD

You're more likely to survive at sea on a boat than on a life raft, so don't rush to abandon ship. Even if your boat is damaged, you're almost certainly better off onboard. Why? Because the bigger the boat, the more visible it will be to a rescue party, and the better protected you are from the wind, water, and sun.

PROPER PROVISIONS

If you have to leave your boat because it sinks, then your life raft should be equipped with a basic survival kit. This will include a shortwave radio, a GPS receiver (a Global Positioning System receiver that can calculate your exact position in the ocean), a compass, a knife, self-igniting flares, a waterproof watch, a waterproof flashlight, warm blankets, a box of matches in a waterproof container, a first-aid kit, and some dry food. However, the most important thing you should have onboard is fresh water. A lack of fresh, clean water will dramatically reduce the number of days you can stay alive.

Warning: No matter how thirsty you get, NEVER be tempted to drink seawater. Seawater is three times as salty as your blood, and your body would not be able to cope. It would also make you extremely thirsty.

You will also need to eat. There should be provisions in your raft, but once these are used up, don't panic. Fish should be plentiful in the ocean, and flying fish may even land in your raft. If you don't have a fishing rod, try using twine and hooks made from wire or aluminum cans.

You can eat the flesh of fish raw. Don't forget to eat the eyes as well. It may sound gross, but these contain water, too. Just make sure you don't eat the organs or you may become sick.

STAY DRY

Seawater is your number-one enemy, so your main goal should be to keep dry and stay warm. If you are out in cold weather, you could develop hypothermia (a condition that sets in when your body temperature drops below its normal level). This can be deadly within a very short time period. If you're adrift in hot weather, exposure to seawater and sun can damage your skin, leading to blisters and other infections.

THE BOYS' BOOK OF GREATNESS

If your life raft has a canopy, use it. If not, try to rig up sheets and blankets as a shelter from the waves and from the sun as soon as possible. If you remain exposed, you will survive for a shorter time than if you are undercover.

STAY OR GO?

Even if you know your location, attempting to row toward land may not be your best strategy. Currents and riptides may push you farther from your destination, and your efforts to row the life raft may waste precious energy.

If your boat was able to send a distress signal before it sank, staying close to where you sent the flare will mean that you are more likely to be found by potential rescuers.

SIGNAL AND SURVIVE

A survivor in a life raft will be almost invisible in the vast ocean. As a result, it's important to be ready to signal to any passing plane or ship. If you have self-igniting flares and a shortwave radio, make sure you know how to use them so you are ready to swing into action at any time.

If you don't have either device, use a handheld mirror to reflect sunlight toward rescuers, or attract attention by using a whistle or a flashlight. As a last resort, waving brightly colored material may also be effective.

Warning: Before setting out on a voyage, always tell someone your route and the time you will arrive at your destination. This way people will know where to look if you don't arrive.

HOW TO MAKE
AN ICE CREAM FLOAT

Like ice cream? Like soda? Well, there's an easy way to double your enjoyment by making your very own ice cream float.

You Will Need:
• an ice-cold glass • chocolate or vanilla ice cream • Soda (cola works best) • a spoon • a straw

WHAT YOU DO

1. Pour cold water over the outside of a large glass, then put the glass in the freezer. Leave it for around fifteen minutes, or until the thin layer of water on the outside of the glass freezes.

2. Take the glass out of the freezer and add two scoops of chocolate or vanilla ice cream.

3. Pour cola slowly into the glass. It will fizz and rise, so don't rush it. (If the bubbles start to overflow the top of the glass, place your index finger on the rim of the glass to burst them.)

4. Grab your spoon and dig in. Use your straw to reach the soda at the bottom of the glass.

HOW TO BE A ROCKET SCIENTIST

You can make sure your career as a rocket scientist takes off using a few things you can find around your house.

You Will Need:

• some water • effervescent, soluble antacid tablets • an empty plastic 35-mm film container with a tight-fitting lid (ask for spare ones at a film-developing store)

WHAT YOU DO

Fill a quarter of the film canister with water (too much water will make your rocket too heavy to lift off, so experiment to get the right amount).

Head outside because firing rockets is messy!

Put one of the antacid tablets in the container and quickly seal the lid tightly. Place the canister on the ground, lid side down.

Stand back and watch as your rocket launches into the sky.

Warning: Do not stand directly over your rocket or you will find yourself in the line of fire.

20

HOW TO PRESERVE A TOOTH

If you or a friend has a tooth knocked out while playing football, soccer, or in an accidental collision, don't panic. These simple steps might help you preserve the tooth long enough for it to be refitted by a dentist. You'll soon be smiling again.

1. Find your tooth! Don't touch the root. Hold it by the "enamel," which is the hard, white outer coating.

2. Run home. Clean your tooth thoroughly, rinsing it in milk (not tap water) to remove any blood, dirt, or grime.

3. Find a clean plastic container with a lid and put the tooth in it. Cover the tooth completely with milk.

4. Take the tooth (and yourself) to your dentist as quickly as you can (within one to three hours of the accident). If you've followed these instructions, you'll have a fifty-fifty chance of having your tooth successfully refitted.

HOW TO PERFORM A PERFECT ROUND-OFF

A round-off is a more impressive stunt than a cartwheel, but it takes a bit more skill and practice to master. It starts off exactly the same as a cartwheel, but you should bring your feet together while you are upside down and land facing the direction you came from.

Follow the steps below to perfect your round-off. Make sure you practice on a gym mat or a similar soft surface.

1. Start with your right foot forward if you are right-handed (left foot forward if you are left-handed). Extend your arms above your head as shown.

2. Lunge forward, placing both hands on the mat, one after the other (as if you were going to perform a cartwheel). Kick your legs up, one by one, until they end up side by side stretched vertically above your head for a moment.

> **Tip:** Be prepared to absorb the impact of your landing by bending your knees slightly as your feet hit the mat. If you find yourself off-balance when you land, add a small jump rather than a step, as this will look like part of the move.

3. Twist your body as you snap your legs back down to the mat.

4. When you land on the mat, you should be facing the direction from which you came. Your round-off is complete.

HOW TO ESCAPE FROM A FIRE

Fires are rare but they can be deadly, so make it your job to make sure everyone in your household knows exactly what to do in an emergency. Here are some useful tips.

BE PREPARED

Appoint yourself the fire marshal of your household. Insist that your home has well-positioned smoke alarms fitted around the house (at least one on each floor). Check each alarm at least once a week to see that the batteries are working. Never, ever let anyone in your family "borrow" the batteries from the alarms to use in toys or other appliances.

FIRE!

As soon as you become aware that there is smoke in the house, make sure everyone is awake and ready to get out of the building quickly. Do not stop to take anything with you.

If you can get out through a door, touch it with the back of your hand before opening it. If it is cool, it's probably safe to open it and go through. Turn your face away and then open it a crack to make sure.

Smoke and fumes rise, making the air down by the floor clearer and easier to breath, so crawl to an exit on your hands and knees.

Once you're through, shut the door behind you. This can slow down the progress of a fire by as much as ten minutes.

If the door is hot when you touch it, take an alternative route to safety. If you're heading out through a window, make sure you know how to open it. If you need to break the glass, cover it with a sheet, a towel, or a pillow first. Protect your hand and arm with fabric as well. Smash all the glass out of the frame so you don't cut yourself climbing through the window.

If you are trapped in a room with running water (the bathroom or the kitchen), soak towels, curtains, pillowcases, or blankets in water and stuff them into any cracks that are under the doors or between the floorboards. This will stop smoke from seeping into the room.

Call 911 as soon as possible. Once help arrives, let the professionals do their job. Once you are outside, get as far away from the building as possible. Let a firefighter know if everyone is out of the building or if you think there may be others still inside.

HOW TO TIE A CLOVE HITCH

A clove hitch is one of the most useful knots you can learn. It will allow you to attach a rope to almost anything. Use a clove hitch to moor a boat, secure a rope when rock climbing, or simply to attach a piece of string to a paper clip!

Practice the simple steps below to attach a piece of rope to a rock-climbing clip or carabiner.

1. Make two identical loops with your rope.

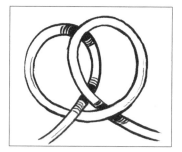

2. Slide the loop on the right in front of the loop on the left.

3. Open the carabiner's gate (the clip part) and lift the two loops through the gate.

Pull both ends of your rope down to tighten the clove hitch.

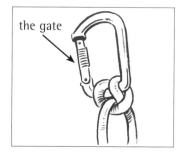

the gate

26

HOW TO BE GOOD AT NAMING CAPITAL CITIES

Have you noticed that geography tests, TV quiz shows, and general knowledge questions nearly always ask about capital cities? Impress everyone with your exceptional knowledge by memorizing this list of capital cities.

Australia – Canberra

Canada – Ottawa

Chile – Santiago

China – Beijing

Ethiopia – Addis Ababa

Finland – Helsinki

Ghana – Accra

Iceland – Reykjavik

India – New Delhi

Indonesia – Jakarta

Jamaica – Kingston

Lithuania – Vilnius

Mexico – Mexico City

Mongolia – Ulaanbaatar

Nepal – Kathmandu

North Korea – Pyongyang

Poland – Warsaw

Russia – Moscow

South Korea – Seoul

Tanzania – Dar es Salaam

United Kingdom – London

United States – Washington, D.C.

Uruguay – Montevideo

Vietnam – Hanoi

Wales – Cardiff

Zimbabwe - Harare

HOW TO BE A MEMORY MASTER

If you've been getting dates wrong on your history tests or if your puppy is starving because you forgot to buy its food, don't worry. Here are some ways to turn yourself into a memory master.

PRACTICE MAKES PERFECT

Play this game with your friends to keep your memory in great condition. Before your friends arrive, collect twenty objects and put them on a table. Here are some suggestions:

• a pencil • a plastic toy • a DVD • a mug • a sock • a fishing rod • an ice-cream cone • a cell phone • a stone • a key • a paper clip • a baseball cap • a book • a spoon • an apple • a sugar cube • scissors • a ruler • a watch • a yo-yo

Now cover all the objects with a cloth. When your friends are gathered around, lift the cloth for twenty seconds. Then cover the table again and get everyone to write down every object they can remember. The person who remembers the most items wins.

MEMORY TECHNIQUES

Here are some tips to help you remember things:

• Ever wondered why you can remember sports scores but not the name of some old king? It is the joy (and misery) that you experience following your favorite sports team that makes it easier to remember their triumphs (and defeats). Try to attach some emotion to the information that you need to remember by finding out some more interesting details. For example, Prince Albert of Great Britain died of typhoid in 1861. His widow, Queen Victoria, wore black every day until her own death forty years later. By knowing that fact, you will be far more likely to remember the date of his death.

• Try to make memorable mental pictures of things you need to remember. For example, if you keep forgetting to feed a pet, imagine it doing something crazy like nibbling the roof of your house. This visual image will pop into your mind, triggering your memory.

• Rhymes and memorable sentences are great ways to make remembering information easier. Here's a useful way to remember the names of all the planets and their order in the solar system, starting with the planet nearest to the sun. (In case you were wondering, Pluto is no longer officially a planet.)

My Very Educated Mother Just Served Us Noodles.

The first letter of each word in this sentence is the same as the first letter of each of the planets:

Mercury, Venus, Earth, Mars, Jupiter, Saturn, Uranus, Neptune.

Try making up sentences for other things you need to remember.

HOW TO BE A YO-YO STAR

Once you've mastered the basic up-and-down yo-yo motion, it's time to turn on the star quality as you master a sleeper, throw a forward pass, and walk the dog. You will need a good-quality yo-yo and some serious practice to master the moves described below.

THE SLEEPER

The idea of the sleeper is to gain enough control of your yo-yo that, instead of bouncing back up to you, the yo-yo "sleeps."

Hold the yo-yo in your palm with the back of your hand facing down. Bend your arm up toward your shoulder and, as you straighten it, smoothly release the yo-yo from your hand, flicking it out and down toward the floor with your wrist.

When the yo-yo reaches its lowest point, keep your hand still for a while. This will ensure the yo-yo "sleeps" at the end of the string, still spinning but not coming back up.

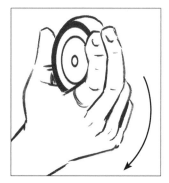

After a few seconds, turn your hand face down and jerk the yo-yo back up.

THE FORWARD PASS

Hold the yo-yo in your palm with the back of your hand facing up. Instead of dropping the yo-yo toward the floor, throw it out horizontally in front of you. When it reaches the end of the string, jerk your hand to bring it back. Turn your hand so you catch the yo-yo in the palm of your hand.

WALK THE DOG

Throw a sleeper (see opposite page) toward a flat floor. When the yo-yo is "sleeping," lower it onto the floor. As soon as the yo-yo makes contact with the floor, it will start rolling away from you. Tug the string to bring the yo-yo up to your hand.

HOW TO ESCAPE FROM AN ANGRY BULL

Next time you're out in the countryside, keep your eyes peeled and stay out of fields that contain any large, menacing bull-like shapes, especially if that shape is on its own. Bulls are generally happier when they are close to cows. However, if you do find yourself in the middle of a field with an angry bull, here's what to do.

STAY STILL

Don't approach it, and try not to draw any attention to yourself. Though it may be hard, you should resist any instinct to run. A bull can smell and hear better than people, but it can't see very well. If you move, you will attract its attention.

32

Always keep the bull in sight. Once it has moved away from you or doesn't seem interested in you anymore, start heading slowly and steadily toward the gate of the field.

CHARGE!

If it is too late and the bull is heading your way, it's time to run. Bulls are fast movers and can easily outrun a person. As a result, you need to look for cover in a nearby building or behind a solid gate or fence.

As the bull charges toward you, do your best to try to distract him. Take off your jacket and swing it wildly in the air to attract the bull's attention. Then, before the bull gets too close, throw your jacket as far away from yourself as possible. Hopefully, the bull will follow the jacket instead of you. Repeat with as many layers of clothing as you have until you reach safety.

Tip: Don't panic if you are wearing something red. Bulls don't react to red any more than any other color.

Warning: Never walk a dog through a field of cattle. All cattle, especially bulls, hate dogs, and if they spot one they will be far more likely to get grumpy.

HOW TO OPEN A JAR

Impress your family and friends with your strength and skill at opening the most stubborn jar.

HOT WATER

If the lid is made of metal, run hot water over it for about twenty seconds (be careful not to burn yourself). Alternatively, fill a basin with hot water and stand the jar in it upside down, so the water covers the lid completely. Never use boiling water as it might cause the glass of the jar to crack.

Dry the lid thoroughly with a towel. Pull on some rubber gloves (to help you grip) and twist the lid.

OPEN SESAME

If the lid is still stuck, turn the jar upside down and carefully bang the lid firmly on a hard surface. Repeat this two or three times, then twist the lid. It should easily come undone.

Tip: All screw-thread lids open counterclockwise (when viewed from above).

HOW TO BE TOP DOG

Although you actually *can* teach an old dog new tricks, there's no doubt that it's easier to train and improve the obedience of a puppy. If you are lucky enough to get a puppy, this is a great opportunity for you to spend some quality time with the fluffiest member of your family. What's more, by putting in some effort at the start, your puppy will be sure to grow up knowing that you are top dog.

LIE DOWN

1. Get your puppy to sit in front of you while you hold its collar. Have a treat in your hand and show it to the puppy.

2. Lower the treat toward the ground so that your puppy must move its whole body downward to keep its eyes on the treat. Keep ahold of your puppy's collar so it can't gobble up the treat.

3. As your puppy begins to move downward, say, "Down," clearly.

4. If you're having trouble, you can encourage your puppy by gently picking up its front legs and lowering it to the ground. Don't forget to restate the command "down" while you are doing this.

5. Once your puppy is lying on the floor, give it the treat.

6. Keep repeating the exercise, but replace the reward with ear-tickling, neck-scratching, and generally making a big fuss every time your puppy obeys.

GOOD DOG!

• **Short and Fun.** Keep your dog-training sessions short and fun so your furry friend enjoys each lesson.

• **Keep It Simple.** Give your puppy one clear instruction to follow. Remember that it is just a young animal and will not be able to cope with anything unclear. Repeat every task again and again to make sure it sticks in your puppy's memory.

• **Be Consistent.** Your puppy will be confused if you change your mind. So, if your puppy is not allowed upstairs on your bed, make it clear that your dog must not go on the beds – ever!

• **Good Dog.** Be positive and offer lots of encouragement (and rewards) to your puppy. Don't punish bad behavior, but make it clear that it won't be tolerated. Always reward good behavior with plenty of hugs and affection.

HOW TO SURVIVE A TERRIBLE HAIRCUT

If you've ever been on the receiving end of an awful haircut that turns you from "too cool for school" into someone who's "too embarrassed for class," read on for some helpful tips.

• **Take a Shower.** Even the worst hair disasters usually look better after a good soak, shampoo, and dry. At the very least, your neck won't be itchy anymore. At the very best, your haircut might not be as bad as you thought.

• **Get Professional Help.** Go to a different barber or hairdresser to see if he or she can repair the damage.

• **Take Drastic Action.** Turn your crooked bangs and tufty clumps of hair into a crew cut. First, ask your parents if you're allowed to have a crew cut. Then get a pair of clippers and hand them to someone you trust – a crew cut is almost impossible to mess up. You may have cold ears for a while, but at least you'll look cool and save a fortune on hair gel.

• **Get a Hat.** A terrible haircut is the perfect excuse to get your parents to buy you that cool baseball cap you've been asking for. Of course, you'll have to take it off at some point, but then you can blame your new look on hat hair!

HOW TO RIDE A CAMEL

Camels may not be a common sight in North America, but in other parts of the world they have been used for thousands of years to carry goods and people.

Camels' long strides and strong backs make riding them fast and fun. They can reach speeds of up to 35 miles per hour, and camel racing is hugely popular in Australia and the Middle East.

If you're ever given the chance to hop onboard one of these one- or two-humped creatures, here's what you should know.

FIND A SUITABLE CAMEL

Don't even think about trying to ride an untrained camel unless you're prepared to visit a hospital. Find a domesticated camel with a trained handler.

Make sure the camel has already been raked to remove any grit, stones, or burrs that could scratch you. If not, rake the camel with a garden rake.

The saddle should be secured with straps so that it is flexible enough to move with the camel's motion without slipping off. Ask the handler to check that the saddle has been fastened securely and will not fall off when you hop on.

GETTING ONBOARD

Unless you have a raised platform, the camel will have to kneel or lie down for you to climb on. Ask the handler to rest one foot on the camel's front leg to make sure that the camel does not get up before you are ready.

Put one foot in one of the stirrups, then throw your other leg over the saddle. Try to do this with confidence to show your camel you mean business.

Settle yourself in the saddle and be prepared for the camel to stand up. Lean back, as the camel will bring its back legs up first. Then lean forward as its front legs come up.

STEERING YOUR CAMEL

Like horseback riders, camel riders use reins to direct their mounts. Unlike on horses, however, the reins are usually attached to a peg inside the camel's nose. Hold the reins confidently without tugging or pulling them. Pulling them too hard will be painful and will annoy the camel.

To turn right, apply slight pressure on the rein in your right hand. Do the opposite to turn left. Relax the reins when your camel is heading in the right direction because it will become confused if you maintain constant pressure.

Ask the handler to attach a leading rein to your camel. The handler can use the lead and guide your camel while you are learning.

GETTING IN THE SWING

Riding a walking camel is surprisingly comfortable. Unlike horses, camels sway from side to side because they lift both feet on the same side at the same time when walking forward. Always move with the sway of the camel. If you fight the sway, you'll have a hard time staying in the saddle.

Tip: Your camel will respond better if you aren't nervous and jittery, so relax and enjoy the ride.

DISMOUNTING

When your ride is over, you'll need to get your camel to kneel down again so you can dismount. Ask the handler to pull down gently on the leading rein and, at the same time, tap lightly on the camel's front legs with a stick. As the handler does this, you must give the command *koosh!*, which means "lie down!" in camel language. Your camel should obediently drop to its knees.

Once the camel is kneeling or lying, ready for you to get off, stand up in the stirrups and throw one leg back over the hump. Jump or step down.

Make sure you pat the camel to show you appreciate its patience.

HOW TO BE A MASTER OF DISGUISE

Disguising yourself is a useful skill if you want to throw someone off your track or follow someone you know without being recognized. A good disguise will allow you to move around unnoticed. To do this, it's a good idea not to draw attention to yourself. The less noticeable you are, the less time people will spend looking at you and the more successful your disguise is likely to be.

BE PREPARED

Think carefully about what you need to create your disguise and whether it will all fit in your backpack or school bag. You never know when you might need it.

Here are a few ideas for your portable disguise kit:

- reversible jacket or top • hat • glasses or sunglasses
- comb • styling gel • baggy clothes • cotton balls
- stick-on tattoos • fake nose • a wig (make sure your wig is a different style or color from your real hair)

CHANGE YOUR BODY SHAPE

If you're on the skinny side, try to make yourself seem fatter by wearing extra layers of clothing. This will also change the way you move. Stuffing cotton balls in your cheeks will completely change the shape of your face. Be careful not to swallow them, though, or you might choke!

If you're not very tall, try to make yourself seem taller. Wear shoes with heels rather than flat shoes, spike up your hair, and don't slouch. Alternatively, you could always try hunching your shoulders to make yourself seem shorter.

CHANGE YOUR WALK

If possible, ask a friend to videotape you walking. This is a great way to see what other people see. Analyze your movements and think hard about how you can change them.

If you usually bounce along energetically, try to slow yourself down. Walk more slowly and make your movements heavy and clumsy.

If you walk slowly already, practice walking faster. Try walking on the balls of your feet or leaning forward. Ask your friend to videotape your new walk and see if you can see the difference. You can also try taking bigger steps when you walk, or try adopting a slight limp.

CHANGE YOUR SPEECH

The way you talk and interact with other people is often a real giveaway. Try to change small things about your voice, by speaking more slowly or at a lower pitch. Talking in a higher pitch might just make you laugh!

CONFIDENCE IS KEY

The most important thing, however you disguise yourself, is to act natural and confident. Nothing will give you away faster than if you are hesitant or awkward in your new disguise – this will quickly arouse suspicion.

HOW TO TALK LIKE A SURFER

Knowing how to talk like a chilled-out surfer dude is much more important than wearing the right surf gear. If you don't want to be seen as a poser, it's time to brush up on your surfer slang.

gnarly – dangerous or challenging

grommet – a beginning surfer

kook – a bad surfer

mondo – huge

poser – someone pretending to be a surfer

rad/radical – excellent

shoot the curl – to ride through the hollow part of the wave

shred – to surf fast or very well

stoked – excited

wipe out – to fall off your board

HOW TO TIE A BOW TIE LIKE JAMES BOND

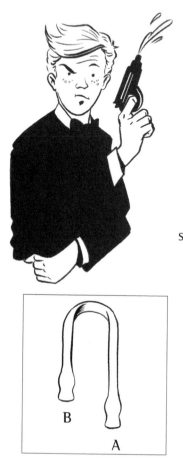

One of the most amazing things about James Bond (after the stunts, the gadgets, and the cars) is his ability to look cool when he's wearing a bow tie. If you've ever tried to put one on yourself, you'll know it's easier to wrestle with all sorts of wild animals than to tie your own bow tie – until now. Follow the steps below to achieve bow-tie perfection.

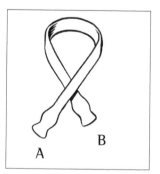

1. Place the tie around your neck, with one end pulled slightly longer (end A) than the other (end B).

2. Now cross end A over end B.

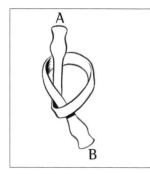

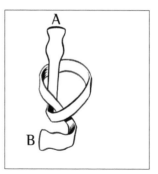

3. Take end A and tuck it under end B and up under your chin, as shown.

4. Take end B and make it into a loop.

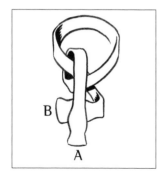

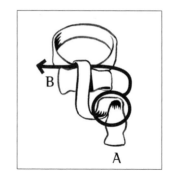

5. Hold the loop with one finger while you bring end A over it.

6. Now double end A back on itself, pushing it through the loop at the back of the bow tie.

7. Adjust both ends and tighten your perfect bow tie.

Mission accomplished.

HOW TO DO SOME DAMAGE WITH THE FINGER OF DOOM

Gather your friends and tell them that you possess a fearsome finger that is so destructive, you can dent cans with it. All you need is an empty tin can (the kind that beans or corn come in), some friends, a bit of practice, and some acting skills.

1. Bring out your tin can and challenge your friends to dent or crush the can in any way using only one finger (no throwing or stamping allowed). The can will remain undamaged.

2. Take the can and lie it on its side on the ground. Inform your audience you will dent it using one finger alone.

3. Put the index finger of your stronger hand across the middle of the can. Then smack the finger with the palm of your other hand. The can will dent, and you can take a bow.

46

HOW TO PERFORM THE BOTTOMLESS CUP TRICK

Here's how to perform a trick that will convince your audience you have a bottomless cup.

You Will Need:
- a full cup of coffee, tea, or another beverage and a saucer • two sugar cubes • a gullible friend

WHAT YOU DO

1. Hold the cup and saucer in your left hand. Hold one sugar cube clearly in your right hand and conceal the other cube under the saucer in your left hand.

2. Tip the cup and saucer very slightly toward your audience, being careful not to spill it! This will ensure that the hidden sugar cube is completely concealed.

3. Drop the cube in your right hand into the cup. The instant the sugar cube hits the bottom of the cup, drop the sugar cube in your left hand onto the floor.

It's all about timing, so practice until you can make it look as if one sugar cube is falling through the "bottomless" cup!

HOW TO HYPNOTIZE SOMEONE

Hypnosis is widely recognized as a powerful tool that can be used to influence the mind and change the way people think. Continue reading to find out how you can hypnotize your friends and get them to do whatever you want.

TEST YOUR SUBJECTS

Figure out which of your friends is going to be easiest to hypnotize. Ask each of them to roll his or her eyes as far up in his or her eye sockets as possible. The farther his or her eyes disappear upward, the better a candidate he or she is.

STARTING HYPNOSIS

1. Choose somewhere calm, quiet, safe, and without any distractions.

2. A person can be hypnotized only if he or she is completely relaxed, so begin by telling your friend to lie down and close his or her eyes. Ask him or her to take a deep breath and, as he or she breathes out, to relax his or her hands, arms, shoulders, neck, head, stomach, legs, and feet.

Always talk in a gentle, soothing voice. The more relaxed your friend becomes, the more likely he or she is to succumb to your hypnotic powers. Don't use props such as a watch or swinging pendulum: They are more likely to distract your subject than hypnotize him or her.

3. Reminding your friend to keep his or her eyes closed, ask him or her to do something simple like move the middle finger of his or her right hand up and down.

Repeat this instruction a few times. If he or she doesn't do it, return to the task of relaxing him or her.

4. If he or she does do what you say, you can move on to make some more powerful suggestions. Here are a couple you could try:

• Tell your friend that a fly is buzzing around his or her ears and see if he or she tries to swat it away.

• Suggest that there is a strong smell in the room and see if his or her nose wrinkles up.

Build up your suggestions slowly and don't make far-fetched requests. Don't jump in and ask him or her to act like a chicken right away, as there is little chance he or she will do it, and a suggestion that's too silly might wake him or her up.

FINISHING A SESSION

To bring your friend out of his or her trancelike state, simply say, "I am now going to count to five. When I reach five, your eyes will open and you will wake up feeling relaxed and refreshed!"

HOW TO FAKE A SCAR

Whether you want to convince your friends you have a terrible scar, or simply need to look the part for a Halloween party, follow these instructions to make a realistic-looking, gruesome, gaping wound. It will require some practice, but it is well worth the effort.

You Will Need:
- makeup remover
- a tissue
- 1/2 cup of hot water
- a packet of unflavored gelatin
- a Popsicle stick
- makeup (red blush and foundation that matches your skin tone)
- makeup brushes
- red food coloring
- a tablespoon of cornmeal
- cotton swabs

WHAT YOU DO

1. First, clean the area of skin that you want to create your scar on (it is easiest to practice on your leg). Use makeup remover to get rid of any oil or grease. Pat dry with a tissue.

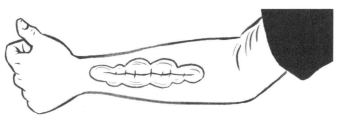

50

5151

2. Mix half a cup of hot water with a packet of unflavored gelatin. Stir with a Popsicle stick until the mixture is syrupy. Allow it to cool a little so it won't burn your skin, then apply a layer to your skin in a rectangle about 3 inches by 2 inches. Let this layer dry on your skin, then apply a second layer over the same area. (Don't leave the gelatin in the cup too long or it will set and be too difficult to apply.)

3. Before the second layer of gelatin mix dries, draw the Popsicle stick across the middle of the layer to create a "gash" down the center. Allow this to dry. You may need to experiment, varying the depth and texture of the gelatin, to achieve a realistic-looking gash.

4. Once the mixture has set, your wound is in place and it's time to cover it with makeup so that its color blends with your skin. Gently pat some foundation on the "scar" and blend it all over the scar area. Be as gentle as you can so you don't dent or flatten the gelatin.

5. Now you need to apply some red blush with a small makeup brush to make the inside of the gash appear pink and sore.

6. Create some fake blood by mixing a few drops of red food coloring with cornmeal and a tablespoon of water. Use a cotton swab to dab the "blood" at various points around the scar. Let it dry.

7. Stand back and admire your handiwork. Be prepared to lap up all the sympathy you will receive for your terrible injury.

Tip: It's a good idea to ask before you borrow anyone's makeup, or you may end up with a real scar!

HOW TO WHISTLE LOUDLY

Whistling a tune is all well and good, but sometimes you can't beat a really loud whistle to grab someone's attention or show your appreciation. Here's how you do it.

1. Wet your whistle or take a drink of water. Learning to whistle loudly can be a thirsty business.

2. Use the thumb and index finger of one hand to make a *U* shape. Leave a small gap between the tips of your fingers. Put your fingers in your mouth.

3. Curl your lips back against your teeth and around your fingers. Leave only a tiny bit of your lips visible. Make sure they are stretched tight.

4. Press your tongue down just behind your bottom teeth. You should have a small bump in the middle of your tongue while the front of it should be wide and flat.

5. Breathe in through your nose and then blow air out through the small gap in your fingers. Use the top of your tongue to guide the air. You may find that pushing down with your fingers on your bottom lip and teeth helps. Keep practicing until you can position everything perfectly and adjust your breath for maximum whistling volume.

HOW TO SLACKLINE

Slacklining is a bit like tightrope walking in that you can impress your friends and family by walking along a narrow, flat rope that's tied just slightly above the ground. However, unlike tightrope walkers (who walk along a taut rope or cable), slackliners walk on specially made tubular nylon webbing, making it a far more exciting and bouncy activity.

First you need to master the technique of setting up a slackline properly. Your local sports store should be able to help you find the equipment you need.

You Will Need:

- three carabiners (these are metal rock-climbing clips with a spring-loaded gate) • two short pieces of slackline or webbing (12 feet long and at least an inch wide) • one long length of slackline (50 feet long and an inch wide)

SETTING UP YOUR SLACKLINE

1. Find two sturdy trees, roughly 15 feet apart.

2. Loop one of the short lines around one of the trees about 18 inches above the ground. Holding the two ends of this line together and using them as if they were one piece, knot them to a carabiner (A) using a clove hitch (you can learn how to tie 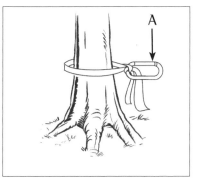 a clove hitch on page 26 of this book). Be sure your slackline is only a few inches off the ground.

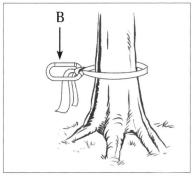

Using the same technique, loop the other short line around the second tree and knot it to a carabiner (B) using another clove hitch.

THE BOYS' BOOK OF GREATNESS

3. Go back to the first tree and knot the long, main line (line 3) to carabiner A using another clove hitch.

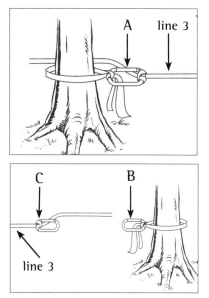

4. Now carry the other end of line 3 back toward the other tree. At a point roughly a foot away from carabiner B, knot a third carabiner (C) to line 3 using another clove hitch.

CREATING A PULLEY SYSTEM

5. Now you need to make a pulley system to control the tension on your main line. To do this, thread line 3 through carabiner B. Then loop the line back through carabiner C.

6. Now make a double loop by looping line 3 again through carabiner B and then through carabiner C. Make sure this second loop fits inside the first loop that you made. Loosely tie the end of line 3 to carabiner C to hold your pulley system in place.

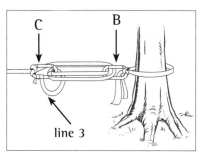

7. Before you try to walk on your slackline, untie line 3 from carabiner C and pull gently on the end of this line. When your line is taut enough to walk on, tie the loose bit of line 3 back to carabiner C to hold it in place.

Experiment with different levels of tautness until you find a level that you are comfortable walking on. If the line is too loose, it will lose its bouncy quality. If you have set it up correctly, your slackline should look like this:

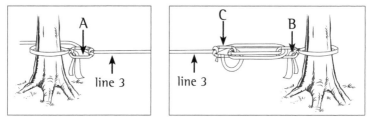

first tree   second tree

WALK WITH CONFIDENCE

Ask an adult to check your slackline to be sure it is secure. Now it's time to learn how to walk the line.

Start in the middle of the line rather than at an end. Get two friends to stand on either side of the line to support you. You'll need to walk barefoot to help you grip the line. Grip the line between the big toe and second toe of each foot.

Keep your head level and look forward, not down. Attempt to balance yourself. Focus on balancing from your hips rather than from any other part of your body.

Put your arms out at shoulder level as though you are imitating a plane. This will steady you a little. However, don't expect the line to be still. It will wobble when you are standing on it, as this is what slacklining is all about. The trick is to let your body move with the movement of the line. If you resist the bounce, you are more likely to fall off.

To start walking, keep your weight on your right leg. Carefully move your left leg out and forward until it is resting comfortably on the line. Then transfer your weight onto it.

Get your balance, then take the next step in the same way. You are now slacklining!

HOW TO KEEP YOUR SNEAKERS FROM STINKING

It takes a lot of skill and effort to make sure your sneakers have that lived-in "street" look. The last thing you want is your mom threatening to undo your hard work by washing them, or throwing them in the garbage because they stink. A few simple steps mean you can have sneakers that look good on the outside and smell good on the inside.

• **Baking Soda.** Put a teaspoon of this in each sneaker and shake it around. Leave overnight, then shake the powder out into the garbage in the morning.

• **Old Socks.** Fill old, clean socks with clean cat litter. Stick a sock in each sneaker and leave them overnight.

• **Tea Leaves.** Try putting loose tea leaves in each sneaker and leave overnight. Shake the leaves out in the morning.

HOW TO BE A VENTRILOQUIST

Ventriloquists use their voices and their powers of illusion to bring a dummy to "life." To become a good ventriloquist, you will need to convince an audience that the dummy is talking, not you. Here are some basic skills you will need to master.

DON'T MOVE YOUR LIPS

It's almost impossible to speak without moving your lips at all, so don't worry if you struggle with this. However, it is important to restrict your lip movements as much as possible.

Sit in front of a mirror and hold a finger to your lips as if making a "shushing" gesture. Say the sounds of the alphabet out loud. You will notice that some letters make your lips move more than others. The worst offenders are usually the letters *b*, *p*, *m*, and *w*.

Substitute these letters with similar sounds that won't make your lips move so much. For example, try saying *d* for *b*, *kl* for *p*, *n* for *m*, and *ooh* for *w*.

This will sound odd at first, but keep practicing and you'll find that you are able to slip these substitutes into words without other people noticing.

DON'T BE A DUMMY!

A ventriloquist's dummy is vital to the success of an act. It distracts the audience's attention from your mouth by looking and sounding funny.

You can use anything from an old doll to a well-loved teddy bear as your dummy. However, a sock puppet (a sock with two eyes sewn on it and a "mouth" operated by your thumb in the toe of the sock) is great to practice with so you can get used to moving the dummy's mouth in time with the words you are speaking.

CHANGE YOUR VOICE

Don't forget that the trick to ventriloquism is to fool your audience into thinking that your dummy is talking, not you. One of the ways to do this is to give your dummy a voice that is different from your own, so practice changing the tone and the speed at which you usually talk. Always practice in front of a mirror so you can observe how visible your lip movements are.

HOW TO HAVE A FOAM FIGHT

Water fights are fantastically wet fun, but imagine a foam fight that ensures everyone gets the frothiest of soakings.

You Will Need:
• a lot of space (preferably a backyard or a park) • some large plastic bottles (caps removed) • dishwashing soap • warm water • baking soda • vinegar

1. Add a good squeeze of dishwashing soap to your plastic bottle. Then fill it three-quarters full with warm water. Add two teaspoons of baking soda.

2. Put your hand over the top of the bottle and give it a good shake so the liquid starts bubbling up. (Never screw on the cap, as this can be dangerous and explosive!)

3. Add a final magic ingredient − a teaspoon of vinegar. The bubble mixture in each bottle should magically turn to foam.

4. Squeeze your bottle to shoot out the foam. Take aim and let the foam fight begin.

Warning: Always avoid squirting foam in your opponent's eyes.

HOW TO "POP UP" ON A SURFBOARD

The key to standing up successfully on a surfboard is learning the "pop-up" maneuver. This is the basic move that helps you get to your feet on your board as quickly and smoothly as possible.

The best place to practice popping up on your surfboard is on dry land. Learning on an unstable surface like a floating surfboard is only likely to take you in one direction – underwater. So, instead of risking constant dunkings, practice on dry land. Take your surfboard, remove the fins (which are usually detachable), and lie it flat on the beach, on the grass in your backyard, or even on the floor of your bedroom.

WHAT YOU DO

1. Lie flat on your board. Begin by doing a push-up, pushing your body up by straightening your arms.

2. Once your arms are straight, jump your legs and feet forward, bringing your knees toward your chest, so you are in a crouching position. If you are right-handed, your right foot should be slightly in front of your left foot.

3. Straighten your legs so you are standing in a sideways position with your feet apart. Your right foot should be near the middle of the board, and your left foot should be toward the tail.

KEEP PRACTICING

Don't stand too upright or lean back, or you're likely to fall over. Instead, try to keep both legs slightly bent. Lean forward a little, and use your arms to help you balance.

If you are struggling to get to your feet, straighten your arms, and with both your knees pulled up toward your stomach, slide your front foot toward the nose of your board.

Keep practicing this move until you can do it in one smooth movement. Once you have mastered how to pop up, take your board out onto the water and try catching some waves.

HOW TO CATCH A WAVE

Before you can impress everyone with your smooth skills on a surfboard, you need to learn the basic principles of catching a wave.

Grab your board and follow the steps below, and you'll soon be catching all the waves.

WHAT YOU DO

1. When you are waist-deep in the water, lie facedown on your board and start paddling out to sea. As you reach the point where waves are breaking, shift your weight forward to lower the front of your board and paddle fast, ducking under the breaking waves. This is called duck diving. Your goal is to pass the place where the waves are breaking and get to where they are starting to form a swell.

2. Once you're in position, stop paddling and sit astride your board slightly nearer the back than the front. Wait until you spot a wave that is big enough or traveling fast enough to pick you up and carry you.

3. As the wave approaches, turn and point your board toward the shore. Lie flat on it and start to paddle. Don't let your body get too close to the nose of your board, because you may push it underwater. As you feel the wave lifting and pushing you toward the shore, paddle as fast as you can.

4. As the wave carries you forward, stop paddling. To keep your board moving as fast as possible, raise your chest a little to shift your weight back. However, do not lean back too far, as this will slow you down.

5. Once you've caught a few waves, you're ready to begin standing up on your surfboard using the "pop-up" move you learned on pages 61 and 62.

Warnings: Go in the ocean only if you can see a green flag flying on the beach. This means there is a trained lifeguard on the beach and it is safe to swim. Keep to the area between the green flags.

Always make sure you stay out of the way of other surfers if the water is busy. They will not be pleased if you cut in on their wave.

Never go surfing alone, and be sure to return to the beach before it gets dark.

Do not go into the water if there are NO SWIMMING signs, if there's a red flag, or if there's a warning of strong currents.

HOW TO RIDE A WAVE

Once you've mastered catching waves and popping up on your surfboard, you need to learn how to ride a wave.

Surfing standing up is all about riding along the front of a wave while staying parallel to the beach. This allows you to surf faster and for longer. It takes a lot of practice, but here are some tips.

• Once the wave has begun to carry you forward, pop up to get you on your feet.

• To keep going as fast as possible, you need to travel along the unbroken part of a wave (not the white water). To do this you will need to steer your board in the right direction. Begin by keeping your body low by bending your legs and adopting a crouching stance. Position your front foot in the direction you want to travel and lean your weight slightly onto this foot.

• Try to keep most of your body weight over the middle of the board to keep you from falling off.

• Focus your eyes on the part of the wave you want to ride.

You're surfing!

HOW TO CALL LIKE TARZAN

Everyone knows that Tarzan is the king of the jungle, and is famous for wrestling crocodiles and swinging from trees. But he is most famous for his amazing jungle call. Here's how you can re-create Tarzan's distinctive call and perhaps even summon a few animals.

Find somewhere you can practice without disturbing your friends and neighbors (it also might be best to make sure you're not close to a zoo, just in case). Fill your lungs with air, then make an "ahhhh" sound from the back of your throat.

After a couple of seconds, gently beat the top of your chest with your fists. This will cause your voice to change, creating a yodeling effect. Beating different areas of your chest will make different sounds.

Try to maintain the call for at least ten seconds, and vary it by changing the flow of your breath.

HOW TO BE A DARING DARTS PLAYER

Hanging a dartboard on your bedroom wall and practicing your throwing technique will get you hitting the bull's-eye in no time.

Follow these tips on how to become a darts champion.

GET A GRIP

Different players grip the shaft of a dart in different ways, so experiment to find the grip that is most comfortable. However, all grips follow the same principles:

1. Hold the dart with your thumb on one side and two fingers on the other. Keep your other fingers folded and out of the way.

2. Keep a light grip on your dart. If your fingers show any whiteness at the tips, your grip is too tight. Too much pressure will make it harder to throw the dart cleanly.

3. Hold your dart straight and parallel to the floor at all times. Never point it down or up.

BODY POSITIONING

Your body position is important, too. Stand slightly sideways to the board with your throwing arm closest to it. Place one foot in front of the other. Your leading foot (the same side as your throwing arm) should be at a right angle to the line behind which players stand to throw their darts. Position your other foot behind to balance you, but keep your weight over the leading foot.

YOUR RELEASE

Aim your dart at the board, concentrating on the spot you want to hit. Bend your arm. Then extend your arm so that it is straight. When your arm is fully extended, release the dart by snapping your wrist. Only your shooting arm should move. Your shoulder should remain completely still.

At the end of your release, your throwing fingers should be pointing down in the direction of the floor.

Keep the release movement smooth. Don't spin the dart by rolling it through your fingers.

If you find the weight of your body falling to one side after you have released the dart, your body isn't balanced correctly. Close your eyes and try to hit the bull's-eye with a dart. Shutting your eyes will help with your balance as you will be able to feel which parts of your body are moving. Be careful to only try this when there's no one else around, though!

BULL'S-EYE!

Once your release is going well, you are ready to start playing a game of darts.

Get a friend to play with you. Each player begins with 301 points. Take turns throwing three darts at the board. After each round, count up how many points you have scored and subtract the total from 301.

Keep subtracting until one player's score is zero. The first person to reach zero wins the game.

Warning: The tip of a dart is very sharp. Never throw a dart at another person or animal.

HOW TO FAKE A SPILLED DRINK

Here is an excellent practical joke that will temporarily cause panic at the dinner table.

You Will Need:
• a paper cup • white glue • red and yellow food coloring • an old plastic bag • scissors

WHAT YOU DO

1. Take a cup and pour in about a tablespoon of white glue. Add a few drops of food coloring to create the look of orange juice. Stir.

2. Spread the plastic bag out on a flat surface. Tip the cup on one side and dribble glue out of the cup to make the shape of a liquid spill on the plastic bag. Make sure the cup is resting on the plastic bag and touching the edge of the "spill." Let the glue set.

3. Once the glue is dry, cut around your spill with scissors.

Wait until the table is set for a special occasion, then position your spill. Wait for someone to discover your "accidental" mishap!

HOW TO POWER A LIGHTBULB WITH A LEMON

Everyone talks about green power, but here's a little "yellow" power. Read on to discover how you can turn on a lightbulb with a lemon.

You Will Need:
- a large, fresh lemon • a zinc screw about 2 inches long
- a copper screw about 2 inches long • a set of unlit old Christmas tree lights • a pair of pliers

WHAT YOU DO

1. First of all, you need to get the juice flowing inside the lemon by gently squeezing or rolling it on a hard surface. Don't break the skin, though, as you don't want any juice to escape.

copper screw

zinc screw

2. Screw the zinc screw into one side of the lemon and the copper screw into the opposite side. Don't screw them all the way through, and don't allow them to touch each other in the middle. Leave them so that the ends of the nails are about an inch apart inside the lemon.

3. Use the pliers to snip one of the Christmas tree lightbulbs off from the set. Make sure you leave about 2 inches of wire on either side of the base of the bulb. Ask an adult for help with this.

copper screw

zinc screw

4. Now carefully peel away about an inch of the plastic insulation from the light's wires to expose the metal wires beneath.

5. Once the end of each wire is exposed, wrap one bare end around the zinc screw.

6. Dim the lights in the room and close the curtains or blinds. Quickly wrap the bare end of the other wire around the copper screw.

7. Look carefully and you'll see that the bulb has been illuminated by the lemon. The acid in the lemon juice creates a chemical reaction when it touches the metal, producing energy. This energy is enough to light the bulb.

HOW TO SKID YOUR BIKE

Skidding the back wheel of your bike (also known as a side skid) is a simple but effective stunt you can do with just a little practice. It makes for a pretty impressive entrance.

BEFORE YOU START

• Your bike should be in good condition, with the tires pumped up and with good treads on them.

• Your brakes should be working well, and you must wear safety gear, such as elbow and knee pads and a helmet.

• You need a hard surface for skidding, so choose an unused stretch of asphalt or a concrete area at a playground. Make sure there are no other vehicles using the area before you attempt a skid.

PERFORMING A SIDE SKID

1. Start by pedaling fairly slowly, traveling roughly the same speed as a slow jog. Don't worry if this seems a bit slow; once you've mastered the technique, you can go faster.

2. Move your weight forward off the back wheel and lean slightly to the right as if you're about to go around a corner.

3. Take your right foot off the pedal, and hold it straight out to the side. Keep it just above the ground. Then brake hard with your back brake. (The back brake is usually operated by the brake on the right-hand side of your handlebars, but it can vary.)

4. You should feel the back tire trying to grip the ground, and the bike will begin to rotate, skidding to the left. As your bike comes to a standstill, put your right foot down to steady yourself.

5. Practice the side skid, building up your speed gradually, for a more impressive and longer-lasting skid.

HOW TO FOOL YOUR FRIEND

Try this trick on your best friend and see what happens.

You Will Need:
- 2 cups of cornmeal • a large mixing bowl • water
- a quarter • a wristwatch or stopwatch

WHAT YOU DO

1. Pour the cornmeal into the bowl. Slowly add some water and stir the mixture until it has a thick, custardlike consistency.

2. Invite your friend into the kitchen and show him or her the mixture.

3. Ask him or her to give you a quarter and produce one of your own. Drop both coins into the bowl.

4. Now challenge your friend to put his or her hand in and grab one coin within five seconds. If he or she manages to do it, he or she can keep both coins.

5. Time five seconds and see how he or she does.

THE VICTORY

You will find that the quicker your friend attempts to grab the coin, the faster and harder the mixture will set around his or her hand. This should make it impossible to fish out either of the coins.

To show your friend how it is done, put your hand into the mixture very s-l-o-w-l-y, find a coin, and slowly pull it out.

Tip: Practice your technique beforehand to get your time down to five seconds or less. Remember, the slower your hand moves around in the mixture, the easier it will be to fish out the coin.

HOW TO GO CRABBING

Crabbing's a great thing to do if you're on vacation near an ocean or a tidal river. It's easy to master, and you can normally catch crabs without a lot of special knowledge or fancy equipment.

You Will Need:

• a piece of string or fishing line • a metal hook (the top of a wire coat hanger will work) • a nut or bolt • bait (from a bait shop) • a bucket • a small fishing net

WHAT YOU DO

1. To make your crabbing line, tie the hook to the end of your string or fishing line. Tie the nut or bolt to the line directly above the hook to weigh the line down.

2. Find a good spot for crabbing, such as near a bridge or pier. Unlike fish, there are usually plenty of crabs to go around, so you don't need to find an isolated spot.

3. Fill your bucket with water from the sea or tidal river.

4. Bait the hook on the end of your crabbing line.

5. Drop your baited hook into the water and let it sink to the bottom, keeping a tight hold on your end of the line. Wait for a few moments for your weight to settle on the bottom.

6. Wait patiently until you feel a slight tug on the line. Then bring your line up slowly until you can see if anything is on the end. If you've been successful, you will have a crab clinging to your line. Reach down with your fishing net and transfer the crab from the hook into your bucket of water.

Remember that crabs are living, feeling creatures. You should always treat them gently and lower them back to where they came from once you have caught them. Don't throw them back, as you might hurt them, and don't leave them on the shore where birds may eat them.

Tip: See how many crabs you can catch, or have a race with your friend to see who can catch the most in twenty minutes.

HOW TO BE A JIGSAW GENIUS

It's Christmas and your house is full of relatives. Someone empties thousands of tiny pieces of a particularly puzzling jigsaw puzzle onto the floor and challenges you to complete the picture. If you want to solve the puzzle by New Year's Eve, follow the steps below.

1. Give yourself enough room to take every piece of the puzzle out of the box.

2. Prop up the box close to you so you can see the picture. This is the biggest clue to helping you solve the puzzle, so make sure you can see it clearly.

3. Find all the pieces with one or two flat sides. These will form the edge of the picture.

4. Build the border of the picture first (this is usually rectangular), using up all the edge pieces you have found. This will allow you to get an idea of the shape and size of the puzzle.

5. Place all the remaining jigsaw pieces outside of the edge you've just put together to keep yourself from getting confused.

6. Now group together pieces that are a similar color. Refer to the picture and figure out which areas of the picture these pieces might belong to. They might be sky, clouds, or water, for example.

7. Collect pieces that are distinctive. For example, these might be parts of a bright red car or a yellow boat. Start building this section of the puzzle.

8. If you get stuck, look at the picture for any outlines, lines, or shapes that link several pieces. These might include windows in a building or something like a crosswalk or pavement edge in an outdoor scene. Start building this section.

9. Signs or wording are usually easy to pick out, so focus on finding these pieces. They should be easy to put together and place in the approximate position within the border.

10. Don't get discouraged. If you are really struggling, try grouping the remaining pieces into groups of similar shapes. Then, if you know the shape that a piece has to be, you can try out all the correctly shaped pieces one by one, until one fits. Good luck!

Tip: Take regular breaks from working on the puzzle. Often if you return to a puzzle a bit later, you will immediately spot the missing piece you thought you would never find.

HOW TO MAKE AN EDIBLE IGLOO

Build an igloo out of sugar cubes instead of blocks of snow. Your hands won't get cold, and you can always feed it to a horse when you're finished.

You Will Need:
• a box of sugar cubes • a circle of cardboard 6 inches in diameter • 2 cups of confectioners' sugar • 3 tablespoons of water • waxed paper

BUILDING YOUR IGLOO

1. To start, build the bottom row of your igloo by placing sugar cubes around the edge of the circle of cardboard. Make some icing "cement" by mixing together the confectioners' sugar and water. Then spread the icing on the side of each cube before you add it to the existing structure. Don't forget to leave room for the entrance.

2. Now start building around and up, adding a layer of icing on top of every cube. Stop for about twenty minutes after each row is completed to allow it to dry. You should build up about eight layers of sugar cubes. Stagger the cubes, making each row a slightly smaller circle than the last.

3. Make the entrance arch and flat roof of the igloo separately. Build them on a flat surface, lined with waxed paper, to prevent them from sticking to the surface you are working on. Let them harden for a few hours until they are completely dry, then peel them off the waxed paper.

4. Once you have applied the top layer of icing to the unfinished igloo, carefully position the arch, adding some more icing to fix it in place. Now gently place the roof on top of the other layers. Leave to dry.

5. Place your igloo on a plate. For a finishing touch, sprinkle it with confectioners' sugar snow and decorate with Arctic figures. An edible igloo makes a great Christmas decoration, so why not give it to your mom when you're finished with it?

HOW TO BLOCK A PENALTY KICK

You're the soccer team's goalie and a penalty is awarded against your team. Don't panic. If you don't save the penalty, everyone will understand, but if you do save it, you'll be a hero. Here's how you can become a legend.

• The rules say you are not allowed to move off the goal line before the ball is struck by the player taking the penalty kick. So jump up and down on the spot with your arms and legs spread wide apart. This will make you as big a target as possible, and hopefully it will also distract the kicker.

• Watch the kicker's body language as he or she prepares to take the shot. Look carefully to see if his or her eyes give away which corner of the goal he or she intends to aim the ball at. Stand slightly off-center in the hope that the kicker will aim for the slightly larger opening, and you'll know which way to dive.

• Watch to see if the kicker is nervous or confident. If he or she is nervous, he or she is likely to hesitate or make a weak shot. If he or she is confident, he or she will probably try to show off by kicking it over your head. If you know it's coming, get ready to jump high to save the ball.

• If the kicker is right-footed, he or she is likely to strike the right side of the ball. This means the ball will be aimed toward the center of the net or to the left-hand side, so aim your dive accordingly.

• Always, always dive. Even if the ball is blasted down the middle, you may save it with your legs or feet. Dive just before the ball is struck. It will be traveling so fast that if you dive after the ball is kicked, it will be in the net before you have any chance of making a save.

With a bit of luck you will leave the field as the "Player of the Game"!

HOW TO AVOID LIGHTNING

You're walking to school on a sunny day when the sky suddenly darkens and a thunderstorm is unleashed. Follow this advice to stay safe:

• As soon as you see a flash of lightning, start counting. Count how many seconds it is before you hear the thunder (saying the word *elephant* between each number you count will help you be more accurate). Take the number of seconds and divide it by five. This will tell you a very approximate indication of how many miles away from you the storm is. Five seconds equals one mile.

• If thunder follows the lightning by less than twenty seconds, then you are near the center of the storm and you should take shelter quickly.

• Avoid sheds, convertible cars, trees, or flagpoles. If possible, get inside a large, enclosed building.

• Once inside, stay away from the telephone, water faucets, and electrical appliances such as the TV or computer. These items act as conductors, and the lightning's electric charge can travel through them. If you touch a conductor that has been struck by lightning, the electric current produced will then flow into you.

• If you can't get safely inside and are in an exposed area such as a field or beach, here's what to do. Remove any metal objects, such as watches, rings, or necklaces, and throw them away from you, as these, too, can act as conductors. Kneel down, placing your fingers, knees, and toes on the ground. Bend your head low to the ground and wait for the storm to pass.

HOW TO BE A SOUND-EFFECTS WIZARD

A sound-effects engineer can play tricks with your ears by creating a convincing sound to accompany an action. If he or she has done the job well, you will not suspect any deception has taken place.

Do you have what it takes to become a sound-effects wizard? A real sound-effects engineer will have a range of complex electronic equipment at his or her fingertips and a studio to work from, but you don't need either of these. The key to producing great sound effects is being creative and using whatever is around you to create the noise that you need.

Here are some convincing sound effects you can generate using simple everyday objects. Try some of the following stunts on your friends and family and see if they fall for your sound effects.

• You are out in the backyard when you and a friend spot a huge beetle walking along the ground. As your friend looks away, pretend to step on the beetle (make sure you don't really do it, though). As you step, scrunch a bag of potato chips hidden behind your back. Your friend will believe you have actually stomped on the beetle.

• Your mom hands you an important letter to drop in the mailbox on your way to school. As your mom turns away, bring the edge of the letter up to your lips and blow hard – so your breath rushes along the front and back of the letter. At the same time, move your hands as if you are tearing something in two. If you get it right, the sound you make should be the same as if you had ripped the letter in half. Wait for the look on your mom's face.

• Complain to your dad that your brother or sister is annoying you. Move so you are standing directly between your dad's line of vision and your sibling, then turn and slap your own forearm sharply. Your dad will be convinced you have hit your brother/sister. Be careful with this trick, though. It may sound so realistic that your dad might not believe it was just a sound effect!

• As your friend sits down in a chair, rub your hand across an inflated, wet balloon. The sound will undoubtedly make your friend's ears turn red from embarrassment.

HOW TO TELL A GOOD JOKE

Some people are able to tell any joke and get their audience to laugh. How do they do it? Follow these dos and don'ts and you may figure it out.

DO

• DO know your joke back-to-front and inside out. How many times have people started to tell you a joke and then stopped because they can't remember the story or the punch line?

• DO pace yourself. Never rush through your joke. Be confident and enjoy telling it. Your audience will share your enjoyment and be more inclined to laugh at the end.

• DO keep your jokes fairly short. It's very hard to hold an audience's concentration for more than two minutes.

• DO be confident. Keep your delivery lively.

• DO make the punch line strong. Try to stay confident right through to the end of the joke. Your audience is waiting patiently for the killer ending that will make them roar with laughter, so don't let them down by flubbing the punch line.

• DO build up a collection of good jokes. Copy any joke from friends or professionals that makes you laugh, and adapt it to suit you.

DON'T

• DON'T try to tell jokes in strange accents unless you can do them really well. At best, your accent might confuse the audience. At worst, it might offend people.

• DON'T tell just any joke. Choose one that suits your audience and their interests.

• DON'T be put off if your audience doesn't like your jokes. Listen to the parts they do laugh at, and next time leave out the parts that people booed.

HOW TO BEAT THE CLOCK IN THE MORNING

You never know when you might need to get dressed in a hurry. The next time you've slept through your alarm, these tips will save you valuable seconds.

• **Choose Your Clothes the Night Before.** Everyone's a bit slow and sleepy in the morning, so choose what you're going to wear when you're wide awake and save time rooting around in your closet while you're half-asleep.

• **Take Your Clothes Off Carefully.** If you have to wear a shirt and tie for school, loosen your tie but keep it knotted and hanging around your shirt collar. Undo the top two buttons of the shirt, keeping everything together. Tomorrow you can pull both over your head in a hurry.

• **Keep Layers Intact.** If you're wearing a T-shirt and sweater, always pull both off at the same time, not one by one. That way you will be able to pull them on again together the next morning.

• **Put Out Your Socks and Underwear.** This will ensure you don't leave the house with one red sock and one blue sock on.

• **Keep Some Clothes On.** If it's cold, just keep your socks on at night. It will be one less thing to do in the morning!

HOW TO BE A KUNG-FU KING

One of the most famous moves in kung fu is the high kick. Practice in front of a mirror or try kicking a cushion suspended at chest height. This will allow you to improve the speed, power, and accuracy of your kick.

Here's how you can sharpen your kicking skills:

• Stand at a 45-degree angle to your target. Position the leg you are going to kick with just behind your hips and the other leg just in front. Seventy percent of your weight should be resting on your back leg.

• Transfer your weight forward onto your front foot, keeping your back as straight as possible. As you do, lift your kicking leg with the knee bent. Pivot on your front foot so your raised knee is pointing directly at your target. Lift the knee as high as you can (at least as high as your waist).

• Aim to hit your target with the top part of your foot. Do this by straightening your leg rapidly in a kicking motion.

• Once you have made contact, quickly return to your starting position.

Warning: Never aim a high kick at anyone else, except in self-defense.

HOW TO GET IN AND OUT OF A HAMMOCK

A hammock is the perfect place to relax and swing gently in the shade. Unfortunately, getting in and out of a hammock can be the very opposite of relaxing. It's easy to end up flat on your back and red in the face. So follow these expert tips to make sure you stay cool at all times.

GETTING IN

Grip both sides of the hammock and pull the middle area of the cloth taut.

Don't jump on. Instead, lower your bottom onto the area you are holding taut. Rest your weight on your bottom, then lean back slightly, keeping your feet on the ground.

Once your back is on the hammock, slowly swing your legs off the ground and into the hammock.

Try to lie at a slight angle, with your head at one side of the hammock and your feet diagonally across it on the other side.

GETTING OUT

When you've woken up or it's time to get out of your hammock, the first thing to do is to turn on to your side.

Slowly move your legs over the edge of the hammock and lower them until they touch the ground.

Hold on to the front edge of the hammock with both hands.

As you transfer your weight from the hammock to your feet, push the hammock away from underneath you.

If you've timed it right, you should find yourself on your feet with the hammock swinging away from you.

HOW TO RECOGNIZE DEADLY SNAKES

If you're traveling to a different country or to another part of your own country that is known for its venomous snakes, it's a good idea to be able to recognize these ruthless reptiles.

If you do come across one, stay calm and try to move slowly out of the snake's range. If you are bitten, get medical help immediately. Being able to identify the snake that bit you may just save your life, as it will help the paramedics decide which antivenom you need. Carefully read the descriptions of each snake below.

THE INLAND TAIPAN
(ALSO KNOWN AS THE FIERCE SNAKE)

Found In: Dry, arid regions of Australia.
Deadly Rating: This snake's venom is the deadliest in the world. Just one bite can be fatal to a human being.
Nature: Generally inactive but will attack if provoked.
Appearance: These snakes

can grow up to 5 1/2 feet long. The back, sides, and tail are often pale brown in color, but the rest of the body is usually black in winter and dark brown in summer.

THE AUSTRALIAN BROWN SNAKE (ALSO KNOWN AS THE COMMON EASTERN BROWN SNAKE)

Found In: Australia, Indonesia, and Papua New Guinea.

Deadly Rating: This snake is responsible for more deaths in Australia than any other.

Nature: Aggressive.

Appearance: These snakes can grow up to almost 6 1/2 feet long. They are mostly brown and can have a range of patterns on their backs, including multicolored bands and speckles. They can move very fast. When angry, they hold their necks high in an S-shape.

THE MALAYAN KRAIT (ALSO KNOWN AS THE BLUE KRAIT)

Found In: Southeast Asia.

Deadly Rating: The Malayan krait's venom is fifteen times stronger than a cobra's.

Nature: Timid during the day. More aggressive at night.

Appearance: This snake can grow up to 5 feet in length. Its back has black and white bands that widen as they reach its white underside. The head is grayish, with lighter lips. This snake will often hide its head within its coiled body for protection.

THE TIGER SNAKE

Found In: Southern Australia, Tasmania, and their coastal islands.
Deadly Rating: If untreated, more than half of bites are fatal.
Nature: Aggressive if threatened.
Appearance: Tiger snakes grow to about 5 feet long. They often have bands, like a tiger, but range in color from yellow and black to olive- and orange-brown with a paler underside. If threatened, tiger snakes make a loud hissing noise and will raise their heads like a cobra to strike.

THE SAW-SCALED VIPER

Found In: The Middle East, Central Asia, India, and surrounding areas.
Deadly Rating: These vipers are responsible for more human deaths than any other species of snake.
Nature: Aggressive and quick-tempered.
Appearance: They grow to about 3 feet long and have short pear-shaped heads with large eyes. The scales on their lower sides stick out at a 45-degree angle. When threatened, the snakes form C-shaped coils and rub them together, making a loud sizzling noise. They move quickly with a side-winding action.

HOW TO TALK LIKE A PILOT

If you've ever listened in on a pilot's conversation, you'll know they use a special system to spell out words. It's known as the spoken phonetic alphabet and is used to avoid confusion during intercom conversations. Learn the alphabet below by heart so you can use it in emergency situations or when it is important for you to be understood.

A – Alpha	H – Hotel	O – Oscar	V – Victor
B – Bravo	I – India	P – Papa	W – Whiskey
C – Charlie	J – Juliet	Q – Quebec	X – X-ray
D – Delta	K – Kilo	R – Romeo	Y – Yankee
E – Echo	L – Lima	S – Sierra	Z – Zulu
F – Foxtrot	M – Mike	T – Tango	
G – Golf	N – November	U – Uniform	

Here are a few useful words that might come in handy:

Mayday – "Help!"
Roger, Over, and
Out – Ends a conversation.
Sit-rep – Stands for "situation report," such as "Where are you?", "Is anybody injured?", etc.
Ten-Four – Confirms you have understood the message.

HOW TO LOOK AROUND CORNERS

You can use a homemade periscope to look around a corner or to make sure you get the best view at the movies when the biggest kid in town is sitting in front of you.

You Will Need:
• two juice cartons (wash them out and let them dry before using them) • scissors • a marker • a ruler • two small rectangular mirrors • strong tape

WHAT YOU DO

1. Carefully cut the top off each juice carton, so each one is squared off.

2. Cut a rectangular opening at the bottom of one of your cartons. Leave about 1/4 inch of carton around the sides and bottom of the hole you have just made.

3. Place the carton on its side with the hole facing you. Lay your mirror

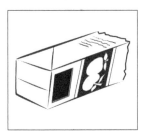

flat on top of the carton so that its longer side aligns with the bottom. Mark a spot at the bottom right-hand and top left-hand corner of the mirror with a pen. Remove the mirror and use your ruler to draw a diagonal line to join the two dots, as shown.

4. Cut along the line you have drawn. Then slide the mirror through this slot. Turn the carton around and look through the hole you've already cut in the front of the carton. You should be able to see the sawn-off top section of the carton in the mirror. Use tape to fix the mirror in place.

5. Now do exactly the same thing with the other juice carton.

Look through here.

6. Turn one of the cartons upside down and place it on top of the other one. There should be a square opening at the bottom facing you and another at the top facing away from you. If you have everything aligned correctly, you should be able to look through the bottom opening and see what's ahead of you. Stick the two cartons together with tape.

Congratulations! You have made a periscope. You will find that what is ahead of you is reflected in the upper mirror, and then reflected in the lower mirror. Hold it horizontally to look around corners, or hold it vertically to look over walls and fences.

97

HOW TO ROLL A KAYAK

Performing a roll involves capsizing your kayak and then rolling yourself back to the surface in one fluid movement. Read on to find out how to perform this manuever.

Warning: Never attempt to roll a kayak on your own. Always learn to use a kayak with an instructor or as part of a supervised class. Wear all the appropriate safety gear, including a helmet and life jacket.

WHAT YOU DO

Hold your paddle out of the water on the left-hand side of the kayak. Lean forward at the waist so that you are lying low and tight against the front of the kayak.

Now, tip your body over to the left side of the kayak, so that you and the kayak roll under the surface of the water.

THE SWEEP

As soon as your body is underwater, lean to your left side again to tip the kayak back toward the surface. Sweep the outboard blade of your paddle (the curved part of the blade nearest your right hand) in a full arc through the water, pushing back and away from the kayak's side.

The sweep will help you roll the kayak while you are underwater, so that you are almost at the surface again.

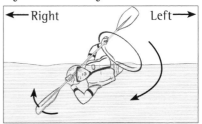

THE HIP SNAP

To bring your body all the way out of the water and your kayak right side up, you will need to perform a hip snap.

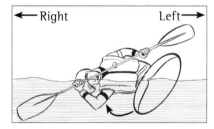

The first part of the hip snap involves rocking the kayak to your left and then back again to your right. To do this, first stretch your waist all the way to your left. Then quickly stretch your waist all the way to your right. To complete the hip snap, jut your hip toward your right side at the last moment, and you should reach the surface with enough force to snap the kayak out of the water.

Your head and body should be underwater at all times when performing the hip snap – if your head reaches the surface before your kayak, your kayak will drag you back underwater.

THE RECOVERY

The momentum of the hip snap should pop you out of the water. Don't try to lead with your head and shoulders, as this will strain your muscles and may push you over again.

Once you're upright, take a quick stroke forward with your paddle. This will help you reposition yourself properly in the kayak.

HOW TO SURVIVE A FLOOD

If you live in or are vacationing in an area that is coastal or low-lying, a flood could potentially happen at any time. It is important that you are prepared.

EMERGENCY KIT

Keep an emergency kit handy. Be sure it's stored somewhere that is accessible and above floodwater levels.

Your emergency kit should be sealed in a waterproof container and should include:

• drinking water in sealed bottles • a medical kit • maps of the area • signaling devices (including a flashlight and a cell phone) • a spare set of clothes • a sleeping bag or blankets • sealed plastic bags to keep your passport and any other important documents safe

PREPARATION

Advance notice of a flood or approaching tidal wave could mean the difference between life and death, so make sure you follow the news on the radio and TV.

On the first day of a vacation you should familiarize yourself with the area in which you are staying. You need to establish a prearranged meeting place on high ground or in a tall, well-constructed building. Make sure that all the members of your family know a route out of the resort that will take them to your prearranged meeting place, avoiding low-lying areas that may flood.

If possible, make sure everyone in your group carries a cell phone at all times and that they have the numbers of everyone else in the group and of emergency services in the area.

TIME TO GO

If you are lucky enough to have advance warning of a flood, prepare to leave your house. An adult should turn off all gas lines and electrical appliances and, if possible, move furniture and valuables upstairs.

Large objects can be carried away in flood waters, and are a danger to you and other people. Move inside or tie down any outdoor objects (such as patio furniture) to keep them from floating away.

Grab your emergency kit and start to make your way to your meeting place. Never try to outrun a flood by jumping in a car and speeding off. The floodwater will move faster than you can.

Don't be tempted to cross a torrent of water that looks shallow. It is dangerous to wade through water that is any deeper than your knees. Moreover, it is very difficult to tell how strong the current is just by looking at it. The pressure of fast-flowing water on your legs can easily make you lose your balance and fall.

If you do get swept up in floodwater, try to grab something you can climb onto. While you are in the water, you are at risk of being struck by debris being carried away by the flood. Another potential danger in some areas of the world can be wildlife, such as snakes and crocodiles, which may be swept along in the water, too.

HIGHER GROUND

Once you reach your meeting place, use your phone to make your position known to the emergency services. Make sure everyone with you understands how important it is to stay there until help comes.

While you wait, ration the food and water you have with you among the people you are sheltering with. Do not allow anyone to be tempted to drink from the floodwater. It will be contaminated and will probably make them sick. Use your first-aid kit to tend to anyone who may be injured.

HOW TO SIGNAL A PLANE

If you've ever watched planes landing at an airport, you may have spotted someone in a neon vest and ear protectors waving their arms at the pilot. These people are called ground controllers, and their job is to guide planes around the airport once they have safely landed.

Ground controllers communicate with pilots using a series of signals that are understood by aviators all around the world. Each signal has to be clearly executed so there is no danger of the pilot getting confused and steering his plane in the wrong direction.

Here are the ten most commonly used signals. So, next time you're at an airport, you'll know exactly what's going on.

Start engines   All clear

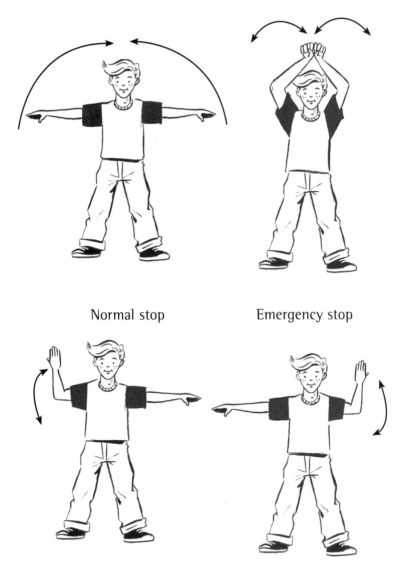

Normal stop

Emergency stop

Turn right

Turn left

Proceed straight ahead

Slow down

Fire
(left arm indicates the
location of fire)

Cut engines

HOW TO MAKE THE PERFECT SNOWBALL

Making a perfect snowball is easy, right? Wrong. Anyone can create a snowball that falls apart too soon or doesn't fall apart at all, but making one that has maximum explosive effect takes skill and practice.

Perfect Temperature. The perfect time to make snowballs is when the temperature outside is around freezing. If the temperature falls below freezing, the snow gets dry and powdery and won't stick together. If this happens, try looking for snow beside your house that might be a little warmer and wetter.

If the temperature rises above freezing, the snow will be too slushy and wet. Look for snow farther away from your house on an exposed area but out of direct sunlight, as this snow should be colder.

Lower Layers. When you locate a patch of good snow, brush off the top layer of fallen snow and use the lower levels of snow that have been packed together. This is perfect snowball-making snow.

PACKING A SNOWBALL

Compression. Start by scooping up the snow and bringing your cupped hands together. As you start to press the snow together, you should be able to hear the squeaking sound of the snow compressing. Don't press too hard, and stop as soon as the ball starts to feel hard.

Add one more scoop of snow and press it around the ball you have already made.

Bare hands are best to make snowballs. The heat from your body helps warm the snow so that it is easier to mold. Throwing it is the only way to truly test your creation. The perfect snowball should "explode" on impact, leaving your target (or victim) in a cloud of snow, with a telltale snowy imprint where the snowball hit.

Warnings: Never aim your snowballs at people's faces, as you might injure their eyes.

Never throw snowballs at moving cars or anywhere near a busy road.

HOW TO PUTT LIKE A PRO

You're out on the golf course, and victory in a tournament is within your grasp. All you have to do is sink a putt. What do you do?

DON'T RUSH

Take time to "read" the green (the smooth, grassy area around the hole). Look for dips, mounds, and other contours. Try to visualize the route you want your ball to take from the moment you hit it until it goes into the hole.

THE RIGHT POSITION

Stand sideways to the hole. Your shoulders should be at right angles to the shaft of your club. Balance your weight equally on both feet to keep your body stable. You should be near enough to the ball to hit it without being cramped or leaning forward. Always keep the blade at the bottom of your golf club flat.

THE RIGHT PUTTING MOTION

Grip the club in the palms of your hands, not with your fingers. Hold it firmly, but don't squeeze, as this will cause your shoulders to tense up, which will affect the smoothness of your swing. Keep this steady grip throughout the putting action to make sure you keep your stroke smooth.

As you take your putt, your shoulders should move back as you raise the club and then forward as you swing your arm to hit the ball. You should not flip or twist your hands when you putt.

THE GLOVE TRICK

If you need extra power for a long or uphill putt, it can be very easy to lose control of your arms and shoulders. To prevent this from happening, tuck a glove under the armpit of the arm that is closest to the hole. You should be able to keep the glove in place throughout the stroke.

AIM FOR A SMALL TARGET

Practicing your putting action is essential. Stick two tees in the ground about 4 inches apart (tees are the small wooden or plastic stands that keep the ball from rolling around before you take a shot). Now aim to putt the ball between them. This is harder than sinking a ball into a hole, because any putts that are slightly off-center will just bounce off the tees. When you're out on the course, you'll find the holes seem much wider and you will be more likely to sink a ball.

HOW TO KEEP A PET SCORPION

Scorpions are popular pets and they are very easy to care for. They usually live for up to six years. If you're interested in keeping a pet scorpion, here are some tips to make sure you stay safe and your pet is always healthy.

CHOOSING THE RIGHT SCORPION

It's always a good idea to do your homework before you buy a pet. Visit a good pet store for advice on which scorpion breed would be best for you. The emperor scorpion is the most popular breed to keep as a pet. The emperor is black in color, can grow up to about 8 inches in length, and has a sting that is similar to that of a bee. Other scorpions that make good pets are Thai black scorpions and Javanese jungle scorpions.

Scorpions are not very sociable creatures, so it is fine to keep one on its own.

THE RIGHT HOUSE

Buy a glass tank with a lockable lid. A 10-gallon tank should be big enough for your new friend.

Scorpions like to live at a constant temperature of about 78°F. To heat your tank, you will need a heated mat (an electrical device that sits just under the bottom of the tank). Make sure you turn the heated mat off if the temperature in your house rises above 78°F in hot weather.

You will need to give your scorpion a regular supply of water. Buy a shallow water container so your scorpion will not drown in it, and add some stones at the bottom for your scorpion to walk on. Scorpions love to burrow and hide away, so add a log to the tank for it to crawl under.

It is important to ask the pet store whether your scorpion is a species that originates in a rain-forest area or a desert area. If your pet comes from a rain-forest area, add a 2 1/2-inch layer of peat-free compost and cover it with orchid-bark chipping. Keep the top layer damp with a daily spray of water. If your scorpion belongs to a desert species, you should add a deep layer (about 4 inches) of sand. (Ask your local pet store for advice on the best type of sand to use.)

THE RIGHT DIET

Scorpions are carnivores, which means they eat meat. You should feed them crickets and mealworms that you can buy online or from a pet store. Feed your scorpion two or three times a week. Always feed your pet at night, as this is when it would normally hunt and eat in the wild.

Warning: Never, ever handle your scorpion – they do sting and it is painful. Some scorpion stings can be extremely dangerous, so if you do get stung, seek medical attention immediately. When feeding, cleaning, or changing the water dish, always wait until your scorpion is away from the lid before you open the tank. Keep an eye on it all the time if the top is open and close the lid quickly if it moves toward the opening. Make sure the lid is locked when you have finished.

HOW TO MAKE A MISSISSIPPI MUD PIE

The Mississippi Mud Pie is a delicious chocolate pie. Its name comes from its likeness to the muddy banks of the Mississippi River, which is close to the region where the pie was invented. To make your own deliciously messy pie, follow the simple recipe below.

You Will Need:
For the Crumb Base: • 1/4 cup butter, melted • 1/2 cup crushed graham crackers • 2 tablespoons light brown sugar
For the Filling: • small saucepan • water • 14 ounces dark chocolate • 1 cup butter • 2 tablespoons boiling water • 1 1/4 cups half-and-half • 1 1/2 cups dark brown sugar • 6 eggs • 9-inch-diameter springform pan (a pan with a removable bottom) • whipped cream

WHAT YOU DO

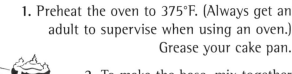

1. Preheat the oven to 375°F. (Always get an adult to supervise when using an oven.) Grease your cake pan.

2. To make the base, mix together the melted butter, crushed graham crackers, and light brown sugar. Spoon the mix into the bottom of your cake pan and flatten it down.

3. To make the filling, fill a small saucepan with 2 inches of water and bring to a boil. Place a heatproof mixing bowl on top of the saucepan. Break the chocolate into the bowl

and stir in the butter and the boiling water. Stir until completely melted.

4. Remove the bowl from the heat and beat in the half-and-half and dark brown sugar. Whisk in the eggs quickly to avoid scrambling them!

5. Pour the mixture into the pan, on top of the crumb base. Bake for an hour and fifteen minutes or until the top is slightly crunchy.

6. Allow to cool before carefully removing the pie from the pan. Top with whipped cream and serve.

HOW TO DRAW WITHOUT LIFTING YOUR PEN

Challenge a friend to draw the number 100 on a sheet of paper without lifting the pencil off the page between each figure. Sound impossible? It's easy! Just practice the steps shown below.

HOW TO RIDE BAREBACK

Ever imagined yourself riding bareback into the sunset like cowboys do in the movies? Before Hollywood comes knocking at your door, you'll need to learn how.

PROFESSIONAL INSTRUCTION

It is essential to learn to ride bareback with an experienced rider or trained instructor. Always wear all the appropriate safety gear. Here are some additional tips.

• Choose a horse with a smooth riding action, a broad back, and low "withers" (the ridges between a horse's shoulder blades). All these factors make it easier for you to stay on the horse.

• Before attempting to ride bareback, practice riding with a saddle but without stirrups. This is a great way to prepare.

• Wear some extra padding in your pants – bareback riding can be painful!

RIDING BAREBACK

1. Use a fixed platform to mount your horse. Once you're astride, take your time getting settled and balanced.

2. When you are ready, take the reins. Set off, making sure your instructor is walking beside you, leading the horse.

3. When you're underway, keep your head up and eyes focused on where you are heading. Don't look down, as this might make you sway on the horse's back.

4. Keep your legs long and relaxed, as if your body is sinking down through the horse's back. Resist the temptation to clench your thighs too much. Avoid digging your heels into the sides of your horse.

5. Keep your back straight. Try not to lean back, as this will push your legs too far forward. If you lean forward, your heels will also be in the wrong position.

6. If you feel you are slipping, don't grip your horse with your legs, because this will only cause it to move faster.

HOW TO BREAK-DANCE

This break-dancing move requires plenty of practice and, more important, a lot of confidence. Once you've mastered the steps below, you can begin to improvise, creating your own personal break-dancing style.

1. Place your hands on the floor a little more than shoulder width apart. Your legs should be spread a little wider.

2. Lift your right hand up and bring your left leg forward to the place where your right hand was.

3. Now bend your right leg behind your left leg, so that your right foot is almost directly under your bottom.

4. Next, you need to uncross your legs, keeping your right leg where it is and swinging your left leg out and under your bottom.

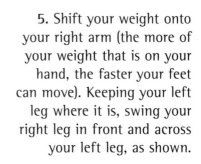

5. Shift your weight onto your right arm (the more of your weight that is on your hand, the faster your feet can move). Keeping your left leg where it is, swing your right leg in front and across your left leg, as shown.

6. Keeping your right hand where it is, step back with your left leg. This is the part you will need to practice to perfect.

7. Now, simply put your right leg back into the starting position and put your left hand on the floor. Now repeat the six steps.

Tip: Don't try to do this move quickly until you can do the steps without having to think too hard. You should soon be able to make it look smooth and effortless.

Now show your crew what you can do!

HOW TO RAPPEL

Rappelling is a great way for climbers to descend a cliff face, mountain, or even a building using ropes. It is used throughout the world during rescue operations, by people exploring caves, and in military activities. Here's some essential advice that will ensure you get to the bottom safely and in style.

Warning: Never attempt to rappel without being supervised. You must learn how to rappel with a qualified instructor, and your equipment must be set up

professionally. You should wear all the necessary safety equipment, including a helmet, safety harness, and ropes.

THE WARM-UP

Go for a run before you start. If your muscles are warmed up before you begin a descent, you will be able to stretch farther and your legs will be able to hold you in place firmly at each level.

THE BASIC MOVE

Once your instructor has safely secured you in a rappelling harness, he or she will then attach a "descender" device through a loop in the center of your harness (a descender stops the rope from moving unless you feed it through with your hand, letting you descend a cliff at your own pace).

When you are ready to begin rappelling, stand at the top of the cliff with your back to the cliff edge. Gently lean back with your legs apart and step off the edge of the cliff. Your rope will keep you from falling. The takeoff is the hardest part of rappelling, so take your time. If you find it difficult, try sitting on the edge of the cliff and gently sliding off.

When both your feet are firmly against the face of the cliff, make a small jump away from the cliff face. As you jump, feed a short length of the rope through the descender by letting the rope slide through your hand. This will let through just enough rope for you to descend the cliff a small distance.

Make your own way down using this technique and taking small, gradual jumps until you reach the bottom.

SAFE DESCENT

• **Choose Your Next Spot Carefully.** At every stage, look down and find a suitable place to land. This should be relatively level and not obscured by any overhanging trees or loose rocks.

• **Make Sure You Are Stable at Every Stage.** Once you've reached your chosen landing spot, use your legs and feet to steady yourself.

• **Take It Slowly.** Rappelling down a cliff face does not in fact involve speed like it does in the movies. Jumping down too fast will put too much pressure on the rope. You may also dislodge loose rocks that could fall on you and injure you.

• **Don't Be Too Ambitious.** When rappelling, make small jumps. Small, controlled jumps are much more effective than long ones. They will give you more time to think about your next move and will ensure you don't make any silly mistakes that could cause you to slip.

If you liked this book, be sure to check out:

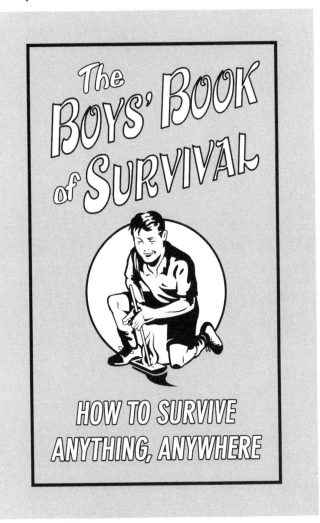

The Boys' Book of Survival:
How to Survive Anything, Anywhere

Treat your family to something **AMAZING!**

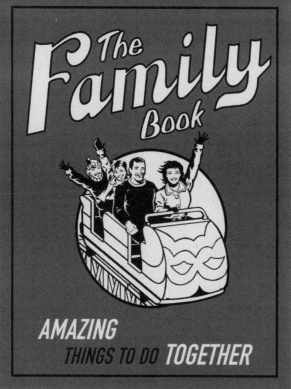

- OPTICAL ILLUSIONS AND MAGIC TRICKS
- MIND-BOGGLING PUZZLES AND RIDDLES
- UNIQUE ARTS AND CRAFTS

And more!

www.scholastic.com

FAMBOOK1